WILD BURRO
RESCUE

A GOLDEN GATE JUNIOR BOOK
Childrens Press, Chicago

WILD BURRO RESCUE

ROBERT FRANKLIN LESLIE

Illustrated by Angus M. Babcock

Library of Congress Cataloging in Publication Data

Leslie, Robert Franklin.
    Wild burro rescue.

    SUMMARY: The author recounts his efforts to save
herds of wild burros in the Death Valley region from being
mutilated and slaughtered by careless hunters.
    "A Golden Gate junior book."
    1. Donkeys—Death Valley region—Juvenile literature.
2. Wildlife conservation—Death Valley region—Juvenile
literature. (1. Donkeys—Death Valley region. 2. Wildlife
conservation) I. Babcock, Angus M., illus. II. Title.
SF361.L47   639'.97'9725   73-496
ISBN 0-516-08872-6

To my dear friend
MARJORIE THAYER

1

THROUGHOUT THE ARID wastelands of the Southwest roam small herds of wild burros, those shaggy little donkeys descended from the beasts of burden brought from Spain by early explorers. When sixteenth-century *conquistadores*—Coronado, de Niza, and others—came to the end of their expeditions, they simply abandoned the burros or traded them to the Indians. Many of these hardy animals escaped captivity, flourished and multiplied, adapting themselves to desert environment as successfully as wild animals. Today we call them *feral* burros, meaning domestic but living wild.

Across the vast expanses of the Southwest these unusually intelligent creatures graze entirely on native desert plants. They are friendly to man. No wonder that in time many of them have become natural companions of the desert prospector, always leading him safely from waterhole to waterhole by their unerring senses of direction and smell. Tales of burro acumen and intelligence comprise a large body of Southwestern folklore.

My own first acquaintance with the wild burros came about when, as a young rookie high school teacher, I used a two-week Christmas vacation to go prospecting in Southern California's Mojave Desert — the Death Valley region near the Nevada State Line. Snow-capped peaks with cactus-studded slopes tower above prehistoric volcanoes and rainbow-colored flows of lava. Much of Death Valley is an awesome, pathless waste of shifting sands, yawning canyons, and rugged buttes —accented now and then by the bleaching bones of man and beast who ignored nature's code.

The Death Valley country is as rich in precious stones and metals as any region on earth of equal size, and that winter I intended to dig not only for gold but for silver and turquoise as well. I had teamed up with an

old-time prospector, a "gulch bum" named Silas Marner Jones, and together day after day we broke our own trail through sagebrush and cactus, searching for treasure.

Camping near canyon springs whenever it was possible, we watched herds of wild burros come in at sunset to drink. I began to notice that many of the jacks and jennies limped and stumbled, obviously suffering from gunshot wounds. As we moved from waterhole to waterhole, we saw more and more mutilated creatures—and carcasses of the dead animals.

Beside a campfire one night Si told me their appalling story. Savage outrages were being perpetrated against these harmless and inoffensive creatures. Whole herds of burros were being deliberately used for target practice by both private and Government aircraft. So-called sportsmen were shooting these tame animals with bow and arrow. Wranglers were using inhumane methods of capture, transportation and slaughter in order to supply processors of canned and frozen pet food. Worst of all, perhaps, amateur marksmen wounded but failed to kill their defenseless prey, leaving them to die in agony.

What Si told me—and what I saw with my own eyes day after day during that Christmas vacation—so shocked me that I made it my business to investigate further as soon as I returned to civilization. At the State Capitol in Sacramento I consulted Fish and Game Commission reports. I read U.S. Department of the Interior's research findings. I talked with Dr. Henry Weber, founder of the Desert Protective Council at Indio.

What I discovered was almost unbelievable. *There were neither laws nor refuges for feral burro protection.* Unenlightened Government officials, both in Sacramento and in Washington, D.C., looked upon wild burros as pests and therefore had declared what amounted to open season for donkey destruction.

My initial anger at such flagrant injustice against animals so harmless and defenseless hardened into a cold rage. But what could one man do? It would take many years and large sums of money to muster enough public support to obtain protective legislation for the endangered herds. I had neither the time, the money, nor the know-how to undertake such a cause. The more I pondered the insolubleness of the problem the madder I became.

Then it came to me—a wild-eyed, cock-eyed plan. There *was* something one man could do—and I would do it. My efforts wouldn't be enough, certainly, but they would help, would be a beginning, might possibly

11

fire others to act.

I could hardly wait for school to close for summer vacation. At last it did and on June tenth I walked into the private office of a veterinarian friend of mine, a man whom I shall not name but simply call Dr. J. He sat behind his big mahogany desk and heard me out while I told the story of torment and untimely death among the back-country burros of the Death Valley region. Then I went on to outline my project: I wanted to take a "clinic" to the burro herds, a "clinic" in a rucksack. Breathlessly, I asked Dr. J. to teach me a quick, condensed course in veterinary medicine and surgery, then to furnish me with the necessary instruments and supplies. I would be a donkey doctor. On future vacations and holidays I would trek into the Mojave wilderness areas and care for as many wounded burros as I could find.

"Leslie, you're nuttier than a fruitcake!" Dr. J. shouted when at last I had finished. "Of all the hairbrained notions! Don't you realize it takes six years of soul sweat to become a vet?"

His glasses jumped up and down on the bridge of his nose as he raved on about the impracticability of my idea. He shot the plan so full of holes that after a while I longed to crawl off and forget the whole thing.

12

Dr. J. fairly ate the air around me as he talked. I began to suffer claustrophobia in his air-conditioned office with no windows.

"I suppose I really didn't expect you to understand," I said bitterly. "You were born inside a fence."

Suddenly Dr. J. jumped to his feet and paced the floor. He chewed his lower lip for a minute, then charged toward a wall of shelves crammed from floor to ceiling with technical-looking books. He pulled out a dictionary-sized volume and thrust it at me.

"Here," he said. "Read this. Memorize it. And don't come back before you know everything in it."

In a daze I read the title: *Principles Of Veterinary Surgery*.

"You'll help?" I managed to ask. My question was almost a whisper.

"If you're nutty enough to go through with this scheme, I guess I'll have to help you. The crazier the caper the more I get suckered into it!"

Sworn to secrecy, I can divulge neither his true name nor the community he serves, but for three months Dr. J. saw to it that I put in a minimum of eighteen hours a day in study and clinical techniques. Assuring me that a young man of my age could get by on three hours' sleep a night, he started in-residence training

13

even before I had finished reading the *"Principles."* He taught me everything from simple bellyache to the most complicated internal surgery. As his assistant I began to operate on dogs, cats, hogs, sheep, goats, cows, horses—and one burro.

Diagnosis and prophylaxis were the most difficult subjects. Anatomy I already knew from a recent college major in comparative zoology. Dr. J. clothed me in starched whites, quizzed and coached me between calls, and addressed me as "Doctor" in front of clients. He had me diagnose every case from simple colic, cuts, and sniffles to complicated intestinal parasitism, infection, tumor, and terminal cancer. There were dire emergencies of toothache, snake bite, gunshot, poison, broken bones, and fight wounds. He breathed down the back of my neck and whispered instructions through operations, bone settings, castings, extractions, and the administering of medicine and anesthetics. He chewed me out later if I had been clumsy or hesitant in the slightest degree.

One Sunday morning at the end of three months, Dr. J. gave me the stiffest comprehensive examination I have ever undergone, then flatly announced that I was ready to achieve my own level of competency in the "boonies." He laid out what looked to me like a fortune in sharp, shiny new instruments, pharmaceuticals, anesthetics, narcotics, and tricky hobbling and muzzling gear. He told me that a number of people, trusted friends of his, were interested in our "secret project" and had contributed enough money to buy what was needed.

"These are the tools of your new trade, Bob," he said at last. "You get no diploma, no license to practice. You'll never collect a fee. You could go to jail for what you're about to do. I hope the satisfaction makes up for the hard work and the risk. An M.D. works on one species that can generally tell him what the problem is. A vet has to know the same amount about a hundred species, none of which can point to the pain or say 'Ah!' to indicate they understand what you are up to. Keep on studying. You've just begun. Get back here every time you need supplies or information. Good luck!" We shook hands.

Dr. J. was the most generous taskmaster that ever turned out a donkey doctor in ninety days. I learned much later that he had been born on an Indian reservation—where there were no fences.

2

I USED MY spare time that winter to build my portable
clinic, a Trapper Nelson pack rack, designed like
those used by the early voyageurs in the north woods.
The canvas rucksack was divided into three separate
sections, each with a zipper. Into the top section went
the heavy manacle-type hobbles, muzzle, and a large
syringe pump. The middle section held an aluminum
box into which I carefully arranged the sterilized
hardware needed in operations: gloves, hemostats,
spreaders, lances, scissors, probes, thermometers,

tweezers, needles, sutures, hypodermics, and numerous technical instruments for specific jobs. The bottom section held an aluminum box filled with anesthetics, drugs, disinfectants, distilled water, absorbents, and a large variety of specific medicines. Fully loaded, the pack weighed forty pounds.

Because of a nickname given by my desert-rat prospecting buddies, in time the pack became known throughout the Death Valley area as the "Rawhide Clinic." No matter what the terrain, time of year, or length of journey, I always carried the pack myself.

My friend Silas Marner Jones owned a board and batten house near Darwin in the Argus Mountains where he worked in a corporation-owned lead and silver mine. A good many regional prospectors worked for the "Company" until they could grub-stake themselves for six-month jaunts into the "cuckle-burs and beggar-ticks," looking for gold. These men paid Si to board their burros in his corral. Some left the area and never reclaimed their stock. One middle-aged jenny called Winkie had come to Si in that way. She had been on every trip we had taken together before Si settled down to a steady job. Because of my new quest into the desert that next Christmas vacation, he made me a present of Winkie.

Winkie had been born into a wild herd—and she was a prospector's dream. Strong as an ox, as gentle as a kitten, she was desert-wise, loyal, dependable, and plain good company. But there was a lot more to Winkie than that. She had every reason to expect to be treated as an equal of man. Being a free-foaled burro, she regarded lead ropes and night hobbles as downright insults. She demanded equal heehaw time at dusk and dawn to rebut the distant burweed cantatas of fellow burros. She expected to break trail between springs because she knew the shortest, easiest routes better than any prospector.

But Winkie's most incredible characteristic came to the fore on the many occasions I used her to decoy wounded burros within lassoing distance so that I could either patch them up or inject a lethal overdose of strychnine or aconitin. I won't make any claims I can't substantiate, but in my own mind I am convinced that she knew from our first encounter with a wild herd that my intentions were honorable—and different from those of other men toward the wild donkeys.

On that first winter trip with the Rawhide Clinic we left a vernal waterhole in the Panamint Mountains known as Dodd's Spring and headed toward the next aquifer in Cerro Gordo Canyon. We had gone perhaps

18

a mile when we came upon a jack and his eight-jenny harem. They had bedded down for the day in a canyon "willow-wallow." Burros often dig shallow sleeping basins in damp willow or cottonwood shade. As we walked into the clearing, the animals sprang to their hoofs, brayed, and focused their long ears in the forward position of curious study. One old mare remained down. At my approach, however, she struggled to her hoofs. She was suffering from having stepped into someone's carelessly discarded tin can, which she was unable to shake off. Her left front hock was badly swollen, and obviously infection was creeping up her leg.

I set the Rawhide Clinic outside any possible arena of struggle, untied Winkie's pack rope, and lassoed the jenny. The tighter she pulled the rope against her windpipe the less she argued about surrender, but her associates glared with fiery expressions—snorting, switching their tails, stomping the sand. Somewhat jittery, I coaxed the jenny across the clearing to the closest willow and cinched the rope so that her head was barely above the gravel creekbed. While she bucked and snapped her cavernous jaws, I clipped the handcuff-type hobble around her knees and entangled her hind quarters so I could drop her to the ground. The unfortunate beast fell onto the sharp gravel with a painful thud. After hog-tying her forelegs to her hind gaskins, I went to the Rawhide Clinic and prepared a hypodermic of pentothal sodium for anesthetic. The herd paced back and forth in a semicircle like caged lions. Sensing danger, Winkie stepped between me and the incensed burros even before the old jenny lost consciousness.

My first task was to cut away the rusty can with my sideknife. Several incisions into the burro's flesh were necessary to drain the infection and treat the affected tissue with a sulfa compound. After sterilizing the cuts with argentol and painting the leg with a strong insect repellent, I removed the rope and shackles. There was nothing more to do but sit and wait for her return to consciousness. When the drowsy burro stood up, she seemed surprised she could now experiment with walking on four hoofs.

Before retying Winkie's diamond hitch, I took from one of her paniers two carefully hoarded oatmeal cookies—one for Winkie who, at a critical moment, had stood between me and the bellicose troupe, one for a grateful out-patient.

We resumed the pathless route toward the Cerro Gordo. Most of that day Winkie walked close to my elbow, which she nudged each time she caught my eye. This was the first of many such encounters, and Winkie's reaction was always the same. The only people ever to assure me that she wasn't capable of expressing elation because we had stopped to help another burro have been those who have never lived with a donkey.

Winkie's eyesight was better than that of most equids. She could see all dimensions of movement near and far. Many a time I aimed my binoculars down her pointing face to discover a coyote that had not yet crept within range of the unaided human eye. Winkie's long, sensitive nose could be trusted whenever location of water was a life-and-death matter—not to mention the number of times she rejected springs that contained dissolved arsenic, copper, and thallium salts.

During the day Winkie never missed a sound, but at night when she lay down she simply switched all consciousness to the "off" position until dawn. To prove she was the world's worst watchdog in spite of her impressive gifts of sight, smell, and hearing, she often slept through nocturnal visits of foxes, coyotes, and ringtails. Wild burros sometimes raided our camp and stole food without disturbing either of us.

As a discriminating animal, Winkie was quick to learn that our partnership went far beyond any beast-to-master bondage. She was never slow in obeying

commands, but she protested if I forgot and shouted at her. On all of our sun-baked treks we shared every cookie, hoecake, orange, and cornflake. At day's end Winkie counted on brushing, currying, and de-ticking. When she licked the top of my head, it was a signal for a neck rub. An elbow nudge meant a quick "eyeball conference," frequently a confirmation that we agreed on some subject such as trail choice, campsite, or weather-maker. Perhaps the most lasting joy both of us derived from this partnership—aside from a remarkable understanding of the other's signals—was a profound sense of mutual trust and confidence which we communicated to each other from our first day together.

3

WINKIE AND I camped one night near a fountain-like aquifer known on a topo map as Ten-Mile Spring— ten miles from nowhere. Late in the afternoon of our arrival, a herd of twelve unusually timid wild burros single-filed past our box-canyon campsite. Winkie and I tailed along at a distance. We stood by until all the burros had watered, except for one big jack with a great blotch of caked blood on his right withers and leg. I headed him up the canyon, threw a lasso around his neck when he turned, and anchored him to a bignonia bush. He was obviously in need of help. Dr. J. had warned me never to allow an animal to drink before anesthesia, especially sodium pentothal or procaine hydrochloride.

With a signal to Winkie to stay with him, I hurried back to camp for the Rawhide Clinic. There may have been some sort of communication between the jack and Winkie, because he allowed me to approach, hobble, and hog-tie him without making any real fuss.

Above the sun-baked, fly-blown blood clot a bullet hole was draining, and, since the slug was still inside, an operation appeared inevitable. To allay his pain and terror I put him into deep sleep immediately, using sodium pentothal together with a muscular relaxant drug known as curare. I estimated that he might have to remain immobilized for as long as eighteen hours in case of lengthy surgery or heavy bleeding.

Considering the jack's weakened condition, the gangrenous stench, and the apparent length of time since he had been wounded, at one point I came very near giving him strychnine sulfate to stop his breathing. But, except for his wound, he was such a prime specimen that I decided to probe for the bullet and to try to kill the infection. His herd refused to leave the canyon without him.

26

In the instrument case Dr. J. had included a long, three-pronged extractor used by doctors for removing safety pins, marbles, and beads from children's lungs. I had never operated the complicated gadget before. First I sterilized it with phenol, carefully inserted it, and, as luck was with both of us, clamped onto the slug and slowly withdrew it—a .38-caliber pistol bullet that had flattened but little. After raking out splinters from the pierced shoulder blade and inducing fresh bleeding to irrigate the wound, I cauterized the deep hole, packed it with sulfanilamide, and sewed the skin loosely to allow serum drainage during healing. I washed the withers and leg with lye soap and an antisepticizing solution, finally dousing the burro's wounded side with carbolic acid to discourage insects for at least a week.

It would be hard to imagine any man who could have remained unmoved had he watched the herd stand guard over the burro while my patient slept through the night. The wild donkeys chased away coyotes, foxes, bobcats, and bighorns, allowing no animal near us or the spring until sunrise.

By three o'clock the following afternoon the big jack was raring to break his fetters and run away, so I injected an intravenous shot of morphine sulphate. He slept until the following morning. Winkie grazed with the herd on wild celery, reeds, and scattered winter grasses. Late that next afternoon I took a critical look at the burro's wound. The leg was so badly swollen that I stood for a long time with a hypodermic syringe in my hand, ready to put him out of his misery.

"I'll bring you a bucket of water first, old boy," I said.

The jack drank two gallons of water and went back to sleep, hardly moving a muscle until daylight. By then the smell of gangrene was gone, swelling was on the wane. When I released him a little later, he walked to the spring, drank heavily, turned and bit Winkie savagely on the back of the neck, then staggered down the canyon to a sage flat where his kin were waiting.

When the donkey herd had moved far out on the desert talus below the canyon mouth, a flock of Nelson bighorns—six ewes, five yearling lambs, and one elegant ram—switchbacked down a game trail and took turns drinking at the spring. The lordly herrenvolk ignored Winkie and me as if we were tumblebugs in a dung heap. For some reason Winkie took a shine to that ram—whose reaction to her was to snub all overtures.

Winkie could stand anything on earth but the cold shoulder. Having fraternized with almost every species of native wildlife, apparently she decided to give the ram a second chance to be friendly. As she pranced like a circus-performing pony around the arrogant bighorn, he and his high-brow entourage stood like sculptured marble, rolling their eyes and turning their heads while the jenny paced around and around. Winkie stopped, walked up to the ram, and began nudging his long, spiraled horns. She pawed the sand in front of him. He continued to stare straight into space without batting an eyelid.

I knew I should have warned her that she was concocting a formula for mayhem, but I was too curious to see how the irresistible would cope with the inevitable.

Winkie finally lay down in front of the imperious ram and rolled over on her back, exposing neck and belly, folding her legs in the appeasement position of a surrendering dog. The ram's only movement was to raise his stubby tail and wiggle it. At this signal four ewes moved into position, two on each side of the naive Winkie. Before I could interfere, the four scored a simultaneous head-whack against the jenny's rib cage and belly. A mountain sheep's horns are no

more than eye guards, so the burro was wounded in dignity only—but I do not wish to minimize that wound. Winkie would undoubtedly hate desert bighorns for the rest of her life.

By the time she had recovered her breath, rolled over, and struggled angrily to her feet, the flock was loping single-file up the switchback toward alpine pasture.

4

Hoping for another look at my convalescent burro when his herd returned for water, I decided to stay close by Ten-Mile Spring for the next several days. It was unusually warm for December, and, while Winkie and I lay in the cottonwood shade drowsing away the late afternoon, a California gray fox meandered down the game trail and crossed the gulch. Cautiously, but with no sign of fear, the wraith-like creature paced back and forth in front of us, his curiosity seeming to exceed the wisdom with which his kind are normally endowed. I can't help suspecting skullduggery whenever a fox appears to attract deliberate attention. Presently this one shot across the canyon, drank from the spring, and just as quickly rebounded to the shade where we rested. He sat down, repeatedly shifting his gaze from Winkie to me. When the burro at last stood up, I thought the fox would leave but, despite the unseasonal heat, the two dissimilar animals ran about thirty feet to the canyon floor, cavorted, rolled, and jumped for ten minutes in the center of the wash, each carefully avoiding body contact with the other.

When Winkie trotted back to the shade and lay down, the panting fox followed her and collapsed full length on his belly, facing her. He gave forth a continuous high-octave whine while I peeled an orange. Winkie affected indifference, knowing she would get the first bites anyway. But the fox actually began to beg as the smell of the fruit filled the air. When I leaned forward and offered him a section, he lowered his head suspiciously, crawled within stretching distance, and finally accepted it daintily. The delectable morsel was entirely new to him, and he bug-eyed in bewilderment when he chomped down on it. A bit of the juice ran down his "Sunday throat,"

33

causing him to cough and to do a corkscrew turn backwards. But he was hooked. After circling the campsite, he slunk back and sat scratching my knee impatiently while I slowly fed him and Winkie the rest of the orange.

The handsome creature never permitted me to touch him, but he bounded around my feet until nightfall, sharing a can of beef stew and a jam sandwich at the supper-time campfire. His bit of skullduggery was all too plain. Sensing me out as a sucker, he had hornswoggled a meal.

It was after dark when a raucous she-fox barked near the spring. In silent, liquid leaps, our friend disappeared. The thought crossed my mind that I should not have contributed to the fox becoming so tame. I had just removed a bullet from a wild animal that had ventured within hand-gun range of the wrong man.

At last the wounded burro and his herd returned for water. The jack no longer limped and, through the binoculars, I determined that he was well on the road to complete recovery. Since vacation time was beginning to run out, Winkie and I left Ten-Mile Spring, skirted Saline Valley's northeastern dunes, and followed an ancient mining road that I hoped would

34

lead to Waucoba Canyon in the Piute Range and a telephone where I could call Si and ask him to collect us in his truck.

At Waucoba Springs where cool, pure water poured from a granite hillside, we met a herd of twenty young burros and an older jenny. It was clear from the moment we entered the willow and cottonwood grove that every burro was under the complete domination of the small middle-aged jenny. Yearlings, having fled the natal herds, frequently—and inexplicably—give allegiance to these little "sagebrush queens." As long as Winkie was at my side the wild burros allowed me to walk among them in order to check for wounds, cholla cactus sections, tick infestations, tin cans on hoofs, or disease. Of all the twenty-one, only the little "queen" was in need of help. She was unable to walk normally because of a football-size tumor alongside her udder. I was frankly frightened to begin work on her. Jacks and jennies alike have been known to fight until death when they consider a leader jenny in jeopardy.

But by some miracle she allowed me to secure halter and hobbles, though when I toppled her she let out a bray that threw her followers into general stampede. They held their heads higher and funneled their ears farther forward than either cattle or horses do on

mass rampage. As they circled closer and closer, the reverberation of their hoofs made me feel as if I were inside a huge kettledrum, but I secured the jenny's four legs and bowlined the long tie-rope to a willow. After picking up the Rawhide Clinic, I urged Winkie to a nearby cottonwood where we stood to await developments. When the "queen" stopped braying, the younger donkeys gradually found hiding places in the dense growth along the streambed.

With a heavy shot of thiopental in her front leg vein, she relaxed into deep-breathing slumber. I untied her before beginning what I had to do. The tumor, a cystic fibroma, had extended no roots into the udder, but it must have irritated her into constant discomfort. While the hour-long operation proceeded without a hitch, I was conscious of scrutiny from every bush. Winkie walked up and down the puny creek as if reassuring the other burros. She came often to the scene of the operation, then returned to the willows.

The little matriach turned out to be my most ungrateful patient. While she was still wobbly on her hoofs and only partially recovered from the anesthetic, she snorted like a faulty steam radiator, biting and kicking each of her own troupe as they came out from behind the willows. Winkie managed to stay out of her

37

way. The jenny would have pommeled me soundly had I not shinnied up a cottonwood and onto a branch out of reach. Her subjects finally surrounded her and hustled her down the canyon toward the mesquite brakes on the open desert drumlins.

Two days later Si picked us up at the mouth of Waucoba Canyon near Independence and took us back to Darwin. It was not until the following December that I was able to get back to Winkie and the desert for more work with the wild burros.

5

ONE NIGHT JUST before the Christmas holidays, Si telephoned to tell me of an emergency near the Lone Willow Spring, a harsh and remote desert wilderness southeast of the Panamint Valley community of Trona. Si reported that an open-range rancher, believing that wild burros were ruining a spring and devastating an oasis, had not only put out poison for them but had enlisted aircraft pilots to help him exterminate the wild herd. As soon as school recessed for the winter holidays, I headed for Si's place at Darwin where he

39

and Winkie were waiting for me.

An old-time prospector friend, a man in his sixties called Boraxo Bill Philander, agreed to go with me to Lone Willow Spring to see if we could possibly drive the persecuted feral herd to another range before the donkeys were completely wiped out. Boraxo had an old burro by the name of Sulfide, an animal with leadership ability when it came to bellwethering other burros. We hoped to use his talent.

It took a full day to grub-stake and make other preparations for the eighteen days we planned to be in the back country. Because of drying winds and no water-table replenishment, springs were habitually in their worst condition in December and January. Each burro would therefore have to carry a five-gallon water can. Winter travel also required sleeping bag liner, jacket, and storm equipment. During those eighteen days the burros would eat a hundred pounds of molasses-rolled oats and carob meal in addition to what remained edible of blackbush and bladdersage. We dared not count on bullrushes and winter *yerbas* at seepages; wild burros and bighorns would have nibbled the last green blade. You could depend upon one thing in Death Valley country—your own gear. There was never a season of natural generosity.

Si hauled us from Darwin to Trona where we began the dusty, run-down, hard-to-find trail to Lone Willow Spring. The day was cool and breezy, the sky vitriol blue, but there were clouds in the southeast. Every hundred yards we saw grim reminders of another generation's struggle with that same land—rusty remnants of a sewing machine, a brass bedstead, a coffee mill, a surrey wheel, a broken slopjar.

Without letting on to Boraxo, who cursed the scene, I thought the surrounding Slate Range mountains possessed a haunting charm. They were bare of vegetation but reflected strange lights, shadows, and violet hazes. Erosion had sculptured the reddish strata into sharp phantasms that resembled an oversized parade of toyland animals from the world of Disney. With Boraxo's practical mind and combustible disposition, he would have "blown his stack" had I intimated that I thought it a pleasant treat to walk between Winkie and Sulfide, imagining that we too were elements in that dream-world parade.

The forty-mile hike to Lone Willow Spring took two days. I was surprised to find many willows and scattered cottonwoods, bignonias, and alders. About six acres of reeds, rushes, sedges, and alkali-tolerant grasses grew along the hillside among the ruins of a

41

former boom town. A nearby ravine led to a desert campsite where a middle-aged prospector, bewhiskered and ragged—but surprisingly clean—was camped with two burros. Boraxo introduced me to his long-time friend, Barnaby Shaw. Barnaby said that two Darwin prospectors, Bean Pole Gates and Down-the-Road Duggin, had passed by and told him about some fool jackass doctor with nothing better to do than operate on "sick uns" in the Panamints and Piutes.

"I hope you got medicine in that Trapper Nelson," Barnaby said with a look that implied my imbecility was taken for granted. "Most o' the sick ones have migrated toward the Owlhead Range where they'll die if they drink the water. Some are wounded. Machine-gunned from Government aircraft. More 'n half the herd's kicked off. You'll smell 'em when the wind changes."

"What about water beyond the Owlheads?" I asked.

"Lots o' water. Leach Spring. Drinkwater Spring."

"Any poison left around?" Barnaby asked.

"I buried what little was left. Jackrabbits were eatin' it and croakin' on the spot."

The next day Barnaby joined us on the eighteen-mile trek to Lost Lake in the Owlhead Range. It was after dark when we set up camp in the sabina juniper near

42

the lake's alkali-crusted shore. At daybreak I rode Winkie halfway around the small lake and found thirty sick and wounded burros lying on the sawgrass. Aircraft gunners had wounded six jennies and two jacks. Of those having ingested poison, twelve were markedly better off than the others. Ten were so sick they could hardly stand up. Diarrhea, either from poison or from Lost Lake water, had reached such a critical state that most anuses flowed blood and mucous. Mouths gaped and tongues, parched and cracked, lay bleeding on the dry sawgrass.

Wild burros were never easier to get acquainted with than those of that desperate band which had fled Lone Willow Spring. Their reason for migrating to Lost Lake remains a mystery, because the water there was not drinkable, and the burros of the region would have known that. Only a few had the strength or the will to raise their heads or lift their ears as we passed among them. Normal herd organization was completely destroyed.

Sensing an atmosphere of trust, I slid off Winkie's rump and crawled on all fours from victim to victim. The look in each bleary eye seemed to me to say, "I'll follow you if you'll lead the way to pasture and drinkable water."

Boraxo and Barnaby watched from the south end of the lake. At a prearranged signal, they brought the Rawhide Clinic and a tie-rope. Without considering the fact that the gunshot victims might not be poison victims as well, we tied and dosed each animal with bismuth emulsion. The dejected creatures put up almost no resistance when we syringed the medicine down their throats—but the job took twelve hours! By ten o'clock that night all the sick and wounded had somehow gotten to their feet and struggled into our camp where they flopped to the ground.

Because of Lost Lake's poisonous water, Boraxo, Barnaby, and I discussed at length the feasibility of leading the herd to Leach Spring about eighteen miles away. I don't think one of us believed we could ever get the burros there, but something irresistible that would not be denied made us decide to try.

Before operating on the wounded, I planned to observe them for a day on the trail. After all, I reasoned, the burros had made it between Lone Willow Spring and Lost Lake. There was one—part of her face had been shot away, two gaping holes in her rump— but the way she followed me . . . . One hopelessly hemorrhaging jenny was unable to get up so I gave her a quick intravenous overdose of veronal.

44

6

THE CURDLED SKY at dawn threatened sleet. The temperature hovered slightly above zero. After feeding each donkey a large oatmeal cookie, a handful of oats, a tablespoonful of salt, and a pint of water, we had no trouble getting each one of them to follow Sulfide's lead. Barnaby and I brought up the rear in a cortege that strung out over half a mile.

It took an hour to descend the Owlshead Canyon below the lake, after which we rested the animals for thirty minutes. When the slow ones caught up, the

band stood in a circle around us and brayed pitifully for more water. Before the burros could become rebellious, Boraxo struck across an open flat of sage and ephedra bush. He led a straight course up the first rocky talus, a pathless route sparcely dotted with creosote bush and beaver-tail cactus. At the top of the talus we followed a dry wash up the deepest canyon of a low saw-toothed range. The veteran "gulch bum" picked a passable route through the boulder-strewn arroyo toward a narrow gunsight pass. Under the weight of the Rawhide Clinic, my own legs felt as if they were at the point of buckling. But I was more concerned for the sick and wounded burros

having to maintain the cruel gait set by Boraxo Bill
Philander.

Strung out now over a mile and a half, the desperate
donkeys kept up their heroic pace. The gusty breeze
had a frosty bite when we faced it. Winkie, sniffing
the clabbery sky, often paused to look back until I
had waited for the little jenny with the mutilated face
to catch up.

Beyond the pass sprawled another talus fan and
thickets of prickly pears. Suddenly we looked down
and saw at the foot of the slope a mile-wide valley—a
green valley—so delicately tinted, so mild in appearance
compared with the surrounding harshness, that it

47

seemed a mirage. On the rich red clay floor grew screw-bean mesquite, bebbia, and sacaton grass, indicating proximity to a water table. Winkie, Sulfide, and Barnaby's two burros grabbed mouthfuls of sweet greens as we crossed the valley, but none of the tag-tail herd wanted to eat. We stopped long enough to give the sick and wounded the last of our remaining water.

Another rugged talus soon lifted us once more into harsh and inflexible desert. We had arrived at the Granite Mountains—twisted, sharp-edged, and tumbled. Corrugated ramparts bristled with cholla and barrel cactus. It was a scene of uncompromising austerity. The last eight miles were twice as bad as the first twelve. The weather worsened. At dark we were still climbing and, according to Barnaby, still three hours away from our destination.

At nine-thirty Boraxo signaled with his flashlight. Leach Spring at last! From a stony, windy esplanade there trickled into a large rock-bound pool clear, sweet water.

When the animals had drunk their fill and dropped to their bellies, we decided to give the second antidote treatment by flashlight. I deferred the necessary surgery until daylight. As tired as we were—cramping muscles threatened to tie us into knots—one by one we hobbled the weary burros long enough to pry open their mouths and squirt thick bismuth emulsion down their throats with a hand-pump syringe. In order to keep from administering the medical ordeal more than once per victim, Boraxo bobbed the tail of each burro treated.

When the last of the stragglers staggered into camp, we counted twenty-four. Six never arrived. The little jenny with only one eye had made it.

After five hours of sleep I prepared to begin surgery in a howling midday gale. Our eyes smarted from sand, alkali dust, and frost. Before pulling on rubber gloves, I turned my cold-numbed hands back and forth above the campfire until my fingers moved normally. Boraxo kept a two-gallon bucket of hot water near each patient so that I could immerse my hands and wrists at regular intervals in order to maintain dexterity with the instruments. I began with the least complicated cases, those requiring local novacaine or at most a numbing shot of nembutal.

The last burro scheduled for general anesthetic was the maimed little creature with rump wounds who had followed me so persistently. Both bullets lay deep within the jenny's lumbar region. I could do nothing for her mutilated face. A 50-caliber slug had grazed her forehead, entered the right orbit, and destroyed the eyeball and cheekbone as it exited.

The jenny was a half-pint-sized tumbleweed, otherwise healthy, plucky, friendly, and perhaps three or four years old. How she had survived machine gun, poison, eighteen miles on the hoof between Lone Willow Spring and Lost Lake, twenty miles of *jornada* (forced march across the desert) to Leach Spring where she had then undergone two hours of major surgery, and finally (during her immediate convalescence) an additional seventy-mile walk, mostly without benefit of trail, across hills, mountains, canyons, and open desert to Trona will always remain in my mind a monumental tribute to donkey courage. Barnaby Shaw named her Miss Cavell, after Edith Cavell, World War I heroine, human yardstick by which female courage will be forever measured.

During our stay at Leach Spring, four of the remaining twenty-four burros died. On the seventh day after our arrival, the weather moderated, so Barnaby and Boraxo prepared to leave in order to spend the rest of the winter prospecting for gold and gemstones in the colorful strata of the Tiefort Mountains. Three generations of prospectors have referred to the brilliantly tinted Tiefort strata as "petrified sleeping rainbows."

50

Both men yearned to "jump claim on that stinkin' Lost Scotty Mine," where Death Valley Scotty presumably took out a fortune in nuggets "the size and shape o' dinosaur eggs."

"Happy New Year, Bob!" Boraxo called as the two men and their burros reached the top of the hill on the morning of their departure. They waved before crossing the divide into the Drinkwater Spring basin.

New Year's Day! Christmas had somehow eluded us.

7

Two DAYS LATER I broke camp to head back toward
Trona. A temporary lull had settled over the desert in
the wind's wake, but the sun failed to burn through
the icy masses of gray nimbus. When Winkie and I
walked toward the brown meadow for a last inspection
of the herd, Miss Cavell ran to meet us halfway. She
knew how fond of her I had become, and it may not
be too great a stretch of the imagination to assume
that she sensed I could never leave her at Leach Spring
for the first cougar or coyote pack to discover that she

had but one eye. When she slipped her head willingly into a hackamore and allowed me to buckle it on her blind side, she voluntarily surrendered forever the feral freedom of open range for a new life of lead-rope and human supervision.

As I led her away, the other nineteen donkeys tried to follow. Their breathing formed a fog-like cloud in the frosty early morning air. They brayed and stomped and nickered—and of course never understood that I drove them back into the mesquite thicket because I wanted them to stay and establish themselves there as an organized herd.

We had no sooner headed down the wash than a penetrating drizzle began to fall. In the Death Valley region, winter may be as frigid as the Arctic or as hot as summer. Leading Miss Cavell behind Winkie, who broke trail, I selected the shortcut route between Leach Spring on the Granite watershed and the shockingly vast elbow region of the Slate Range to the northwest. Icy showers made travel increasingly uncomfortable. Without once complaining about what must have been excruciating pain, never deliberately slowing down, Miss Cavell limped pitifully in favor of her hind leg, croup, and loin where I had operated. Experimenting to determine effective dosage, I gave her an intramuscular shot of morphine to ease her pain. She was drowsy until noon but gradually recovered alertness and a steady step as we moved on at a rate considerably less than a mile an hour.

I had five gallons of water, a five-day food supply, virtually no pharmaceuticals, no trail, and seventy miles of bad weather before the first telephone at Trona. Miss Cavell was the most patient, cooperative, friendly creature imaginable. Her horribly mutilated face belied a keen intellect, unassailable dignity, complete dependability, and an indomitable will to live. But her body could withstand just so much.

Toward evening I made dry camp in a swale that offered some protection from a knify wind. I wove long canes of creosote bush into a mesquite framework to erect a crude shelter like a Piute wickiup. The poncho and Winkie's tarp made a waterproof roof. Both burros wiggled through the opening and lay down before I had finished chinking drafty cracks. When I set the two canvas paniers inside out of the rain, there was barely enough room to squeeze the sleeping bag between the two steamy burros. After giving Miss Cavell a good-night shot of morphine, I crawled in for a crowded but comfortably warm night.

Sunrise through lingering cloud banners was glorious

to behold. A silent storm that night had dropped six inches of snow. The bleak desert landscape was transformed into a panorama of startling beauty and wonder. The sagebrush kingdom with its host of little animals that are always about in early morning now seemed tucked away beneath a beautiful blue-white blanket. The absolute soundlessness gave the impression that only the sun and I were awake.

Miss Cavell, still striving to see with her empty eye socket by turning her head first to one side, then the other, emerged and stared at the surprising white desert. Winkie was still asleep when the little donkey brayed for a second nosebag of rolled oats and sweet carob. I was so elated by her appetite that I began to sing with a flock of gossiping ravens that flew in and walked awkwardly through the snow, pecking and swallowing it as if the desert had turned to sherbet. Winkie sat on her haunches near the wickiup opening and eyed my extravagance with rations—and my tolerance of those abominably noisy ravens who had no better manners than to talk while they ate. As an offering of thanks for the improvement obvious in Miss Cavell's condition, I fed the ravens what I had planned for my next two lunches.

However enchanting both company and landscape

55

were that day, I had to break camp and face the reality of the trip ahead. The closer we came to Trona the easier the going was—and the shorter our rations. Miss Cavell's youth and determination resulted in phenomenal improvement, finally allowing a daily gait of two miles an hour for eight hours.

On January ninth Si drove to Trona and hauled the three of us to Darwin. I stood in the truckbed and held Miss Cavell's head for the entire distance in order to assure her that this new experience was okay, for it was her first automobile ride. I saw a storm brewing in Winkie's eyes as we rode along. When we finally walked into Si's corral, Miss Cavell nudged my chest and nibbled my shoulders in gratitude—for which she received a resounding whap from one of Winkie's hoofs. It was the first time I had witnessed outright jealousy in a burro, but old-time prospectors claim they can never marry because they are afraid of what their jealous burros might do to a bride.

8

AFTER I HAD returned to my schoolteaching, Si treated and entirely cured Miss Cavell's wounds, then found a fine home for her near Hawthorne, Nevada. The last time I heard, she was very much alive and happy as *ex oficio* majordoma on a cattle ranch.

Winkie and I worked together for two more years. As I look back on those days I realize more and more that we traveled not as a man and his donkey, but as a unit. Our consideration, one for the other, on the trail, our habit of walking side by side, terrain permitting, instead of my leading her with a rope, our reciprocal trust, even the sensitive matching of gait—these were the things we grew to share instinctively along a route that was at no time easy or without potential peril.

Winkie never saw the desert's tawny majesty through my eyes. I never saw a bog of needlegrass through hers. What we *did* see together, most truly, was honest response in the eyes of each other—in camp or on the sagebrush trails—particularly if there was a question involving the other's welfare. Our companionship certainly outweighed any temptation Winkie may have had to spend so much as one full hour with one of her own species, even though they were within easy communicating distance most of the time.

What became of Winkie? One night someone forgot to close Si's corral gate and she disappeared. One story had it that rustlers had stolen her to bellwether wild burros into their traps. But I saw her not long ago and we had a grand reunion. I was driving up to Mahogany Flats in Wildrose Canyon. I had stopped the car and had gotten out to look with binoculars at a herd that was bolting up the hillside. Suddenly I thought I recognized Winkie. I whistled and shouted her name. The burro stopped, and the herd stopped too. It *was* Winkie! She ran back down the hill and trotted up to

59

where I stood. First she sniffed carefully, then she brayed, walked on her hind legs, pawed the air, nudged and nibbled me, brayed some more, then licked me across the face. When a car came up the road, she rejoined her troupe of twenty burros whose leadership she had obviously assumed.

Because of hunters, archers, rustlers, and Government-permitted trappers, today the feral burro herds have dwindled. Today free-roaming bands, wary of man the enemy, are indeed wilder and harder to find than their timid mustang cousins. After years of hard work and great expense, some of us finally obtained shaky legislation that protects the wild burro to some degree. Saline Valley at least has been made a burro refuge. But much remains to be done. An Executive order at last forbade target practice from Government aircraft, yet the bodies of dead burros prove that this atrocity still takes place.

Of a winter—and sometimes of a summer—I continue to walk the back-country sagebrush trails between waterholes of the vast Mojave, prospecting for gold. But I have given up carrying the Rawhide Clinic because the wild herds have become unapproachable.

I hope the day will soon come when Rawhide Clinics will never be needed at all. Ecologically sane organizations such as the Desert Protective Council, Defenders of Wildlife, National Wildlife Federation, U.S. Humane Society, and others are carrying the fight to state and federal legislators. But there is still an enormous amount to do before the burro is fully protected by law.

Massive mountain ranges and big-clouded skies— even a few valleys—in the land Silas Marner Jones, Boraxo Bill Philander, Barnaby Shaw and company call home look about the same today as they did when Piutes and Mojaves died there defending their land against white spoliation. Southwest deserts—despite high-speed freeways, airports, housing developments, and "sports"—are just as implacable today as they always were. The air, sun-simmered with yellow sage, rose mallow, and downy lupine, is still delicious to breathe, the song of lark and phainopepla pleasant to hear. And the faraway arcs of sleeping rainbows are splendid for daytime dreams.